Not Forgotten

Not Forgotten

E. B. Grayden

2000
Galde Press, Inc.
Lakeville, Minnesota, U.S.A.

First Edition
First Printing, 2000

Library of Congress Cataloging-in-Publication Data
Grayden, E. B., 1925–
    Not forgotten / E. B. Grayden—1st ed.
        p.   cm.
    ISBN 1–880090–93–7
    1. Aging—Poetry. I. Title.
PS3557.R33385 N6 2000
811'.54—dc21   99–059858

Galde Press, Inc.
PO Box 460
Lakeville, Minnesota 55044–0460

This book is dedicated to my mentor,
my confidante, my friend,
Deborah Keenan

Contents

Foreword   ix

A Woman Named Eve   1

Poems About War   3
    A Day in May   5
    Ink on my Forearm   7
    Marine Reunion 1992   9
    Wartime Cruising   11
    The Sign of the Cross   13
    The Sacred and the Profane   15
    South Pacific Evening   17
    Mary Ann   19
    Coney Island Hot Dog   21
    White Beaches   25

Poems About Death and Grief   27
    First Death   29
    Her Last Wish   31
    Wetness and Tears   33
    Sustained Grief   35
    An Image Journey   37
    The Waiting Room   39
    Today Tomorrow Yesterday   41
    Golden Years   43
    The Grave   45
    The Dream   47

Poems About Family   49
    Her Name Was Mondeh   51
    My Spiritual Life   53
    Blue Eyes   57
    The Fireplace   59
    Forgotten Feelings   61

The Promise   63
Matchless   65
Grandpa   67
Going to Town   69
The Stove   71
Only This Hour   73

Poems About Age   75
On the Age Thing   77
Not Whether   79
Graduation Day   81
The Last Lap   83
Skiing On Aspen Mountain   85
Status Report   87
Thanksgiving 1997   89

Poems About Other Things   93
Cabin Opening   95
The Apple Tree   97
The Lake Place   99
A Plane Wreck   101
Lake Sylvia Storm   103
Spring Break   105
Leaving Loons   107
Vine Hill Leaves   109
Winter   111
Beauty   113
The Pileated Woodpecker Is Back   115
Two Hearts   117
Why   119
October   121
Note in My Mailbox   123
Valentine   125
The Evergreen   127
Still Life   129
Onward Downward   131
Starlight   133

Foreword

This book of poems is about memories of people, places, and things in my life since I was a boy on a farm in northern Minnesota until the present, a span of time covering the Great Depression; World War II; the discovery of wonder drugs, polio vaccine, and antibiotics; the development of transistors and computers, jet engines, nuclear energy, television; the rise and fall of Communism; and an American walking on the moon.

Who else but me and my peers have witnessed such things!

These poems are about my life lived in these remarkable years, but more importantly: these poems are expressions of thoughts and feelings concerning sadness and grief, joy and love, sickness and aging, and the wonder of it all.

A Woman Named Eve

A dowdy, frumpy, plump little lady answered her door to my ring.
With a pleasant smile she invited us in and told us her name was
Eve. Why we were here we were not sure, but friends said we'd
have a ball. We all had heard stories of what Eve could foretell, as
she could hear things from beyond.

She led us into a small sitting room, well lit, and sat in chairs facing
her. Not much chit-chat with this spiritualist. She knew nothing of
us; not our names, where we were from, our ages, our ancestry, or
where we lived. She charged nothing for our visit; a small donation
would be accepted. She told us she was a sales clerk at Dayton's. We
inwardly chuckled—but not for long.

She closed her eyes, expressionless, and just sat there, and just sat
there. She finally opened her eyes and said she had messages for
Bob and my wife, Katie, from relatives who had passed on. She
related the messages together with accurate, detailed information
such as a death by fire and a death by suicide which would have
been impossible to research or fabricate. We were stunned and
numbed, silent and worried.

Eve turned to me and said I was the lucky one; she had seen an
Indian chief on a white stallion in the hereafter, Chief Wildwind,
who has been with me always, saving my life many times—in the

1

War, from accidents, from cancers. He made my life long, prosperous, and happy. He was my guardian angel and is with me always.

I had thought I was just lucky all this time; now Eve had told me why.

Poems About War

Ed Grayden, Staff Sergeant, U.S.M.C.,
back from WW II in 1946, ready to enter
college thanks to the G.I. Bill of Rights

A Day in May

It is Mother's Day and pink petals from delicate apple trees are glorious signposts of spring's entrance into early summer, heralding the first grass cuttings of the new season, road construction, highway detours, lake cabin openings, walleye fishing, the planting of flowers.

So many things to do; so little time left to do them.

The phone rings and a woman's quavering voice tells me I don't know her but she's Mike's daughter, he died this morning of a heart attack, she knew I was a close friend of her father, that we were in the Marines together, he would want me to be his pallbearer, would I?

We said good-bye to the old Marine hero on the rain-soaked grassy knoll at Fort Snelling Veteran's Cemetery. The Marine honor guard fired the three volley rifle farewell salute. Taps were played; the painfully familiar sorrowful haunting notes echoed amidst the multitude of nearby headstones. The casket's American flag, precisely folded, was handed to the grieving widow.

Overhead the crying clouds continued shedding their cleansing tears upon us all.

Ink On My Forearm

How vivid the colors once were, royal blues, scarlet reds, and ocean
   greens.
All sharply divided to make up the eagle, the globe, and the anchor.

Out of the eagle's mouth the unfurled banner with the creed
   "Semper
Fidelis," always faithful. Why tattoo a Marine emblem on your arm?

I have been asked, and I have pondered. Maybe delusions of
   wartime
elitism. Maybe teenage peer pressure mixed in with lots of patriotism

And esprit de corps. Probably stupidity. It was late 1944 and our last
liberty in Pearl Harbor, Hawaii. We had been sent here from com-
   bat to

Rest. We were rested and leaving to attack another island with
   another
funny name, Iwo Jima. We were celebrating our imminent departure.

We stopped at a tent which was a tattoo parlor and watched the
   smiling
Japanese artist sink needles into the young sailor's chest. The boy
   was

Crying with pain. We Marines would never cry. We never did.
Almost sixty years have passed. The colors on my tattoo have faded,

As have I. The eagle, the globe, and the anchor have melted into
each
other. Semper Fidelis remains.

Marine Reunion, 1992

A half-century ago this day these men, gathered here, waded ashore to assault the enemy-held beaches of the island called Guadalcanal.

It wasn't easy, this first campaign; the bloody battle lasted six months and ended in defeat for the foe that knew not surrender. It was our country's first victory, and the beginning of the end of the world's worst war.

Now they are here, these Marines of the First Marine Division, at the famous Iwo Jima flag-raising statue, next to where the heroes lie in Arlington Cemetery. They gather to hear the nation's leaders tell them that the citizenry remembers and is thankful. The old Medal of Honor hero stands with the President, who says, "Well done!"

They come to hear Sousa's music and to stand and cry when the Honor Guard marches in with flags unfurled and flying, while the strains of the "Marine's Hymn" rise through and above the jet noise overhead. The sunny, sultry Virginia air brings back memories of still hotter, more humid days fifty years ago, when all were in harm's way. Where have these years gone, and why so fast?

Memories are everything and everywhere this morning. The old men stare at their counterparts of today; uniformed, tall and hard, straight and proud, stern lipped, with clean-shaven faces and close-cropped heads. They were all like that once, and fifty years from now these young god-like warriors will be wrinkled and aged, pot-bellied, turkey-necked, worn out, with their own memories and the wonderment and sadness of senescence. These Guadalcanal Marines will be bivouacked in Eternity then, but this day is theirs to savor with comrades of a past era, enjoying to the fullest their country's gratitude and homage. Semper Fidelis!

E. B. Grayden, S/Sgt., USMC 429012
First Marine Division

Wartime Cruising

An eerie silence hung heavy in the ship's compartment where the young Marines sat and sprawled on the deck. My heart pounded and I could feel the pressure in my temples as my mind raced frantically. No one spoke but everyone was listening like crazy; ear drums strained to hear the explosion that would kill us all.

It was only minutes, not hours, since general quarters was sounded, turning the ship into a frenetic flurry of running people, all trying to get to their assigned emergency stations at once. A submarine had been detected and suddenly I was transformed into a frightened, shaking coward, knowing I would die at any moment.

Being on a ship at sea, stalked by an enemy determined to blow you out of the water, is a uniquely terrifying experience. There just isn't any place to hide. You can't jump in a foxhole. There is nothing to shoot at. You cannot even give in to panic and run like hell! This ship and this ocean has you trapped and shackled. What a terrible way to die!

Where the hell is the Marine's Hymn now? Oh, God, how did I get into this mess! Tony has his beads out, head bowed, mumbling. Jesus Christ, if you get me out of this honest to God I'll get some beads and mumble too!

The P.A. system blares the all clear signal — it must have been a whale.

The Sign of the Cross

NEVER AGAIN WILL SERBIANS ALLOW OTHER SERBS TO BE SLAUGH-
TERED BY THE CROATIAN NAZI USTASHI—SLOBODAN MILOSEVIC,
PRESIDENT OF YUGOSLAVIA, JUNE 4, 1990.

14,000 U.N. PEACEKEEPERS HAVE BEEN AUTHORIZED FOR CROATIA
WHERE 10,000 PEOPLE HAVE DIED IN THE LAST 10 MONTHS IN A
SERB-CROAT WAR.—ASSOCIATED PRESS, APRIL 29, 1992.

The right hand, open and curled, the forehead touched lightly as
kissed by a mother. The Father. Downward to sternum, brushed

gently in passing. The Son. Now the left breast, then the right,
home of God's shadow. Holy Spirit. Palms together. Amen. Simple,

cleansing, cathartic, soothing. Start anew. The right hand closed,
except for thumb, fore, and middle fingers whose ends touch.

Trinity. The forehead touched gently, as kissed by a mother. The
Father. Now downward to sternum, brushed gently in passing.

The Son. This time the right breast, then to the left. Holy Spirit has
moved. Palms placed together, homage is done. Amen. Simple,
cleansing, cathartic, soothing. Again and again neighbor slaughters
neighbor in the name of the Father, the Son, and the Holy Spirit. One

has the open hand, the other three fingers; one goes right to left, the other left to right.

One a Croatian, the other a Serb.

The Sacred and the Profane

Gray castles and green vineyards look down on snake-like rivers,
sentinels now centuries old. Barges and boats placidly move along
the Rhine and the Moselle
whose enigmatic waters journey toward the distant sea. It is September 1993, we are on "Holiday," sightseeing in the new West/East
Germany.

A village festival in Munster brings forth young and old, bratwurst
and beer, marching bands, folk music, dancing. The crowd sings,
pleasantness is everywhere. On to Arnstad, Erfurth, and Weimar. Verdant parks surround village squares, antiseptic and sterile. Unknown
here: cans and litter. Stern-faced statues on high horses oversee
milling yet quiet people, criss-crossing, not colliding. Vendors display wares quietly, all is in order.

The Church of Saint Lawrence once again stands tall in the city of
Nuremberg. Thin spires reach skyward to kiss clouds that cry.
Birthed seven hundred years ago to be destroyed by Lancaster
bombers avenging London devastation. Now restoration completed, glorious again, born again, as the Christ who is worshiped
within. A testament to the will of the people, to their love of the
sacred, their willingness to sacrifice for beauty and to promulgate
their faith.

The high country of Weimar is thick with green beechwood trees providing solitude and peacefulness to the ghosts of Goethe, Schiller, Herder, and Bach, former residents of this quiet and peaceful area. Other ghosts are also here, in these woods of Buchenwald. Jews and Gypsies, undesirables, residents of the barbed wire enclosure sitting atop this beautiful hill. On the barred, wrought-iron entrance gate still stands the insolent, insulting greeting—*"Jedem das Seine."* (Each to his own.) The smoke of burning cadavers no longer exits the tall brick crematorium smokestack which belched the soot of shame over Weimar, the beechwood forest, over all mankind.

A quarter million ghosts are here amidst the thick trees, surrounding the fifty-meter-high Memorial Tower.

The old, learned priests in Nuremberg discuss with us historical events relating to churches, cathedrals, abbeys, and monks; a murdered pope, a murderous bishop, man's weakness and God's grace. Father Timothy from Ireland tells us Maggie and Reagan are to blame. The Brits took their land in 1920. The IRA is simply fighting to get it back, a just fight. Blowing up restaurants and killing civilians doesn't happen. It's the Brits who fabricate these stories and our controlled media that perpetuate these myths. The IRA only kills Protestant soldiers, enemies of Catholic Irish. Just trying to get their land back. The German Jesuit patiently explains the Balkan problem, who took whose land from whom, and when.

Our rental car speeds swiftly on the Autobahn back to Amsterdam. "Holiday" is over. The clouds have gone, the sky is blue, we can see a hundred miles. It's a great day for a bombing run.

South Pacific Evening

He was uneasy in his sleep. The full moon and the raucous birdcalls from deep in the jungle were prodding the unconscious to become conscious. He did not wish to awaken; he was tired and needed rest. Snatches of dreams and daydreams slipped through his mind like moonbeams through broken clouds, shimmering on the ocean bay, then disappearing. The real and the unreal played tag with him as he lay on his back under the open tent; sea breezes gently stirred the green camouflaged mosquito netting hanging over him. Why didn't someone think of mosquito netting back home? A hot summer evening in northern Minnesota was usually spent in a fitful choice of trying to sleep under hot, stifling sheets, or lying on top; cool, wide-eyed, and frenzied. Why are mosquitoes silent in the South Pacific and sound like a dentist's drill back home? Why do they spread malaria here and not there?

His partially opened eyes looked above his feet. He could faintly see the outline of the enemy-held island of Kolombangara across the bay. He thought of the ten thousand Japanese soldiers there, all probably trying to sleep, cursing their own noisy birds and looking at us. He sees two red camp fires over there, close together. They go on and off in unison, like semaphores aboard ships, signaling one another. Was someone trying to signal? Why would there be lights or fires there at night when all must be blacked out?

Suddenly he was wide awake. Terror and paralysis at once gripped him as he realized those red lights were not fires; they were the eyes of a huge rat perched on his chest, staring into his own!

Mike Marcovich, Mary Ann Gay, and Ed Grayden,
home on leave to bury her brother killed in Okinawa

Mary Ann

Toward evening we stood once more together.

The ghosts of the past awakened in her album by yellowed prints.

Dormant memories unlocked with snapshots taken a half-century

ago.

The high school prom. Her first corsage nestled next to my first

suit. Her brother Tom, my best friend, standing beside me. Timid

Tom, who wouldn't hurt a fly. Across the page lie parched newspaper clippings; stories telling how Tommy died a hero fighting for home and country on faraway Okinawa in 1945.

She had pictures of our mothers who were as sisters, of our fathers, my brother, our spouses, all gone, all dead. Childhood scenes played tug of war with our smiles and tears.

We saw the tiny house nestled near the tall water tower, shiny sentinel for nearby peaks of iron-ore tailings. Fleecy white clouds were backdrops to bold black letters proclaiming to all that this town was Nashwaulk, Minnesota.

Five of us children slept in one bed during our visits. A picture of our old red barn near Duluth recalled her family's visits to our farm. We would lie in our hayloft listening to my mother's bedtime stories of werewolves and vampires, tales designed to frighten us back into the house.

We live alone now, she and I, two thousand miles and sixty years apart. We looked in each other's eyes and slowly kissed good-bye. It was prom night again.

Coney Island hot dog establishment in Duluth, Minnesota

Coney Island Hot Dog

It was a gorgeous September day in Duluth, Minnesota, and the long walk along Superior Street occasioned one nostalgic remembrance after another. I was here attending a reunion of the graduates of Central High School. Fifty-five years had gone by, bringing changes in the town and in us. The fancy pillar-like Radisson Hotel houses a top-floor restaurant with floor to ceiling window walls which slowly rotate, giving the patrons magnificent views of Lake Superior, cigar-shaped ore boats, and the mammoth metal marvel, the Lift Bridge.

Few remember what stood here before. A smoky dark saloon, the Park Inn, haven for immigrant lumberjacks flush with paychecks representing months of twelve-hour drudgery, eager to trade for drunken oblivion amidst a woman's arms.

Also gone from this site was the Holland Hotel, launch site of my Uncle Roddy, lovable, illiterate, a depressed soul in the midst of the Great Depression, searching for escape through the unyielding concrete far below the open window.

Across the street the old train depot still stands, now a museum. A brass band is remembered; cheering friends, relatives waving, teenaged boys leaving home to join the Marines in far off San Diego. We were named the Arrowhead Platoon and many never returned.

This small city on a hill is like a recycled painting with only the frame and glass the same. The shops have different names, facades indistinguishable from those back home, or anywhere else. Where did all the movie theaters go? The Lyceum, Lyric, Garrick, Strand, Lake, and Grenada whose ceiling had blue sky, moving clouds, and blinking stars. I pause beside a corner structure, nondescript in its barrenness, unfitting successor to the old Glass Block Department Store with its five perfumed floors. It was there I first laid eyes on my wife of forty-three years, gone also into eternity.

Suddenly I cross First Avenue East and see a shop with the sign "THE ORIGINAL CONEY ISLAND HOT DOG, IN BUSINESS SINCE 1921." It was still here! Eating here was a rare and remembered experience. I walked through the door recognizing nothing but that special Coney aroma. Approaching the lunch counter, I ordered one from the two waitresses who stood staring at me. I told them how exciting it was for me to find this link to my past, how I used to dream of eating here when I was in the South Pacific during World War II, lying in a jungle hospital feverish with malaria, hoping to get home alive, having a Coney again with my dad. I told them how wonderful it was for me to discover that at least one thing hadn't changed in Duluth all these years.

The waitresses kept looking at me. One asked, "You want mustard?"

White Beaches

It was our first day at Fort Myers Beach. Passing storms had boiling Gulf waves pound the shoreline and deposit fruits of its fury; countless shells cast out and disgorged from the sea's briny bottom an expulsion of marine life and a gift to the many who patrol beaches collecting seashells.

As far as one could see there were people walking and stopping, stooping and digging, collecting their newly discovered treasures. They would be placed on window sills, coffee tables, vanities, dressers; they would be stored in boxes, in attics or garages.

Sprinkled among the many beach people were young mothers watching children run and splash, taking their pictures, feigning surprise and delight when a wet child returned with a newfound treasure.

These young are overshadowed by the many who have heads of gray. They do not run and shout; they walk slowly and bend gently. Most realize they are treading water in the final staging area of their lives from which a last voyage will begin.

Sandpipers skitter and scold among us trespassers who invade their domain. They leave no tracks in the silky white sand on this landscape of whiteness and brightness.

I think of another beach on a faraway island which was just as white and bright. Bloody bodies were lying all over among fox-holes filled with young Marines.

I can't remember seeing seashells there.

Poems About Death and Grief

First Death

I was eight and he was my only uncle, my dad's kid brother, who worked for him. Both were immigrants from Yugoslavia with little education. I loved my uncle, who played with me and made me laugh, especially when he mimicked and mimed my stern and serious father, Big Mike, who rarely played with me.

I never knew what they did for a living, but they drove big cars and drank much wine and whiskey. Other men who worked for my father would come to our house and eat and drink and play with me, but none was as kind and funny as my uncle. When they drank too much they would sing sad Serbian songs and cry for their mothers still in the old country, mothers they would never see again.

Lots of policemen would visit our house. "Is Big Mike in?" they would ask. He would take them into his private room with the sliding wood door. I would open the door a crack and watch and listen. He would laugh and joke with them and give them whiskey and envelopes stuffed with money. Mother told me the night I was born he was in jail and couldn't be with her; he never wanted to be in jail away from us again so he shared his money with them and never was.

Whiskey became legal and the Great Depression took all his property and money. No more fast cars and lady friends for Uncle, who wasn't happy anymore. The newspaper said he jumped from a downtown hotel window and died.

Uncle was the first dead person I ever saw. Two men were beside me viewing him in the coffin; one said people turn to stone when they died. "Look," he said, "just like stone." And he knocked on my uncle's nose. I started to cry and kick his leg until my Mother pulled me away. I never looked at a dead person again.

I miss my uncle; I miss them all.

Her Last Wish

She is quiet, now, her tears have stopped.
They say the tears are from dead brain cells;
they mean nothing. I think not.
She cries when I first come to see her,
when I sit down beside her bed. I hold her
thin, wasted hands in mine. I kiss her forehead.
Wonderment envelops me. I was born out
of this toothless, withered, wrinkled old
woman when she was healthy, vibrant, and beautiful,
full of life. Unknown, then, Lou Gehrig,
unknown Alzheimer. One stole her body,
the other her mind. Her life's greatest fear now
realized; incompetent, incontinent, useless, in this
pastel nursing home. The wall portrait of Jesus stares down
at her. Oh, Christ, if there is a Christ,
why this obscenity? The TV in the corner
shines images of healthy, bronzed bodies dancing,
laughing, bursting with life. Youth is omnipotent.
She's out of it, I tell myself, she doesn't know
you, she feels nothing. Or does she? Her
eyes tell me what she wants. The pillow! Softly, tenderly
over her face! Sweet, kindly death her final wish,
her soundless plea. I tell her I cannot.

Wetness and Tears

Have you ever tried weeping in water? It's unique; it's cool.
First get the water warm, warm as her smile.

Then turn the spray to gentle, gentle as her eyes when
they rest on her sons. Relax and enjoy, relax

and remember. Remember her laughter; remember
her anger. Anger at hunger and sickness and crime.

Think of her speech, and how she loved grammar.
Think of her marching; those protests for peace.

Recall her intenseness; was justice denied?
Recall New York City; her long Greyhound ride.

Now feel the tears swell into your eyes, now
let the sobs come out of your heart. No one

to see you, you're taking a shower. No one to
hear you, no need to stop. The pain is so real

as memories are searing. The tears and the water
both wash down the drain, leaving the body and

soul freshly cleansed. Face the tomorrow as best
as you can; soon you will shower and shower again.

Sustained Grief

Claudius tells Hamlet, "sustained grief is unmanly, and evidence of
impious stubbornness." Hamlet's world had
become "weary, stale, flat and unprofitable."
He thinks of suicide. "To be or not to be."

A year ago this evening she fell asleep beside me never to awaken.
The solace of words from friend and family; logical
acceptance, fails to lift the rusty anchor of sadness and despair
chained deep inside my guts by the certainty of the

irrevocability of death. "Out out, brief candle, life is but a walking
shadow, a mere player who struts and frets his hour
upon the stage and then is heard no more." Our oft-repeated lines
have come to pass.

I sit on the deck of a cruise ship in the harbor of Cozumel under a
blazing Caribbean sun. I see the hotel on the beach where
we once stayed and played. Memories return of our long walks and
talks; tender moments, we were as one.

The ship's sound system softly plays "Maria Elena." Nearby passen-
gers on holiday drink Margaritas, speak irrelevantly while forcing
laughter. Hurry up and have fun, the clock never stops its count-
down to nothingness. Is my grief sustained

because of my loss, or has loss opened the window to the future; it is late and all is in descendency. Adrienne Rich writes of emerging from grief as taking that first step on a long ladder. But where is the ladder?

Katie Grayden, died of
a heart attack in 1991

An Image Journey

The silence in my house is disquieting, unnatural, lonely, frightening, ominous. Sleep is illusory and evasive, unable to block the images that cascade through my mind in a cornucopia of memories.

An owl cries from the woods near my window; is it the same one that caused us to pause and listen, to laugh and to wonder? Now I am alone and the owl only reminds me of her.

The operation is healing quickly. The long, ugly, vertical incision no longer pains; why doesn't grief heal as quickly? And why aren't there grief pills, like pain pills?

An image of cancer cells forms. The doctor said the cells looked mean and ugly. Do they have faces with scowls and pock marks and angry eyes, determined to spread and to kill? If so, then maybe there

are cancer cells that look friendly and apologetic, embarrassed to be the source of concern, willing and eager to be removed or transformed into remission.

A new rain on my roof begins a subtle encroachment into the image journey, as light and as delicate as the new dawn's intrusion into the darkness of my bedroom.

Where has it all gone?

The Waiting Room

Monday evening I sit in the Tennessee hospital waiting room, the one for families of patients who are critically ill, close to death. The room is filled with families who sit in hope while tear-stained sobs are muffled. We all await "the word" from the lord high priest of medicine who monitors instruments and displays, giving orders which mean life or death to our loved ones.

The frail blonde in faded, tattered jeans sobs quietly. My wife comforts her. Her brother may die, she weeps; he's too young to die. I think of my dear brother and wonder when is it not too young? She says her brother never cheated, his wife is lying. Two bullets in the chest greeted him as he came home for supper. Out on bail, the wife sits across the room with family, staring blankly, chewing gum. Her family mingles with the victim's family, talking of heavy rains and crops, calm talk, hushed talk. The young redheaded minister, there to comfort, wanders aimlessly, uselessly, afraid to pray lest he lose. In the corner, CNN blares unnoticed and uncared for, relating deaths by the thousands.

A family name is called out and silence fills the room; the "word" is arriving: thumbs up, or thumbs down? The green-smocked masked one enters and approaches the family.

Today Tomorrow Yesterday

Today is reality. Empty the garbage. Separate the cans from the bottles. Newsprint from magazines. Plastic from glass. Big brother is convincing, trust him. Current events unfold in the daily media maelstrom; what to believe? Not fractured facts; hardened conceptions born of hope, but tempered from living. Why are the good guys so often wrong and the bad guys so often right? Today retirement is a voyage of a frail and leaky boat drifting aimlessly on a lake filled with tedium, boredom, and sameness. The search and struggle have ended, the Holy Grail has been found; it is polycarbonate.

Shakespeare's tomorrow and tomorrow creep; my tomorrows leap, not in petty pace, but in ever-increasing swiftness, faster and faster, like the vortex swirl of soapy bathwater exiting down the drain. Tomorrows bring news of sickness and of deaths; obituaries—increasingly with the little flags—salute the passing of contemporaries whose lifespans shine as yardsticks to one's own mortality. Tomorrows are for dreams and goals yet unfilled; fulfillment is dirty dishes. The fun was in the payment of the mortgage.

Yesterday is rebirth; a time machine to my bidding. Where should I travel this moment? Program the memories and recall excitement, desires, achievements; all enhanced and honed, some imagined. Dead loved ones revisited with the wide-angle lens only age permits. Failures and sorrows and disappointments are filtered, sanitized and softened through the passage of time. In twilight years I think past tense; what has been, the wonder and the joy of it. Today and tomorrow are but a facade of a non-event.

Golden Years

The cool dawn greets the day with sounds of life as Canadian geese fly overhead, beating their wings and honking noisily. Winter's ice is

gone and a pond once again becomes nature's looking glass. Two Mallard ducks paddle aimlessly nearby without a sound, looking for

food, knowing we watch, ignoring us. Songbirds pierce the still air with ageless melody while building new nests or discovering old

ones. Sunrise is promised by the subtlety of dim color appearing on the eastern horizon. Once a railroad track, the foot path stretches

straight as a light beam through verdant marsh and wild raspberry bushes to the far distant highway 101, the halfway point of our four

mile early morning walk. Seldom is the occasion when another walker is met, so unknown, so ignored, this beautiful pristine trail.

Somehow, we felt this was our very own. We walk and we talk, we listen and we observe. No telephone interruptions, no reminder notes

prodding us to do things. Our talks are as a rainbow, with one topic sliding into another. We argue, we laugh. Spontaneity reigns.

We know not that we are happy, and blessed. Many months have passed since our last walk together. She has left me. No kiss good-bye, no list of reminders, no phone numbers to reach her, no itinerary to question. She just left! She vanished before my eyes,

leaving behind a beautiful red-haired mannequin and a dazed grieving husband of 43 years who cries all the time.

I walk alone now in the early morning light, along the same path and observe the same sights and sounds. I long to feel her presence but

I do not. All appears black and white. I talk with myself but my lips do not move; I'm not very interesting. Comfort begins to

surface. I remember my birthday is next week. My twilight years are short-lived.

The Grave

Once again I stand by her grave
on the hilltop beneath the giant maple.
Permanency, stability, and
timelessness surround me. No need to
call that I am coming, or that I can't come,
the grave will never leave. Today is fine,

or next week, or next year. The flowers
I bring will always be welcome. Beethoven's
Violin Concerto, her favorite, will echo
amidst the silent cemetery while I stand and
remember and wonder why I am here
alive and alone while she lies in a hill

under a tree. Every year the ritual unfolds.
The 400-mile journey, then the concerto,
the flowers, a myriad of memories, the welling
of tears. All seem so inadequate and useless.
Thoughts of eternity and enigmatic God's love
clash with feelings of anger, puzzlement,

and bitterness. No answers; the catharsis ends.
Images appear of healthy, laughing children
and grandchildren, of old friends and new ones,
fresh interests, of musty windmills still to joust.

The Dream

I dreamt of my brother last night.

Christmas is almost here again and I wonder

why I haven't heard from him. With the

Vikings losing every Sunday I surely expected

his call. Usually it's within seconds of the

game's ending. I'd pick up the phone and

I would hear that familiar chuckle, knowing

he knew how pissed off I was, and relishing it.

When I called him after his beloved Bengals lost,

he would say, "Oh, did they? I was reading this good book

and wasn't watching." So something must be

wrong! Maybe his kidney transplant is acting

up again. Why hasn't he called? Why

haven't I called? I have this ominous

feeling. I awake in a sweat. I remember

he's been dead almost seven years.

Poems About Family

Her Name Was Mondeh

A portrait of my wife's mother hangs on my wall looking at pictures of my family. Alone and unknown, this pretty young woman stares at her children, her grandchildren, and her great-grandchildren. Her eyes are soft and loving, yet radiate determination and persistence. Hardly any knew her. What a pity.

She came to America near the turn of the century from her Croatian home, searching for her husband, Big John. He had left her and their infant daughter to search for work; he would return with wealth. He never did. She was abandoned. A relative told her he heard Big John was working in a mine in Utah; he would lend her money to search for him.

She somehow found him half a world away in a copper mine in Salt Lake City, and five more children were born. They moved to the mines in Minnesota where she died an early death in 1924 leaving Big John with children ages 14, 11, 9, 7, 5, and 2.

Her life was short and probably bleak. Her portrait knows her legacy.

Big Mike Grayden

My Spiritual Life

They came to America from "the old country," leaving behind friends, family, and religion. They wished to start life in their new home with only what they felt was good. Religion was bad. It must be discarded and forgotten. The Roman Catholics, the Muslims, and the Serbian Orthodox Christians all had the commonality in their teachings of fear and hatred toward one another. Centuries of periodic wars served as sump pumps to the rising poisonous tides of fear, distrust, and antagonism. Harvests of bitter seeds sown by these teachers of Jesus and Mohammed kept their countries in wars and poverty and drove millions to foreign shores searching for freedom, food, and opportunity.

The melting pot found eager ingredients from my foreigner family. They became American citizens and fast friends with Jews, Anglo-Saxons, Scandinavians, good people of many nationalities. Most were immigrants. Unknown here this ethnic cleansing.

Mother convinced Father it would help assimilation if my brother and I were to be baptized in a kind neighbor's church, where hatred and killing were not taught, only love and truth. We were baptized in the First Methodist Church of Duluth, Minnesota, dutifully went to Sunday School, and were started on the long and rocky road to Salvation. My folks remained free of religious beliefs for the rest of their lives—I think.

Once as a young boy riding with my dad on our farm in a loaded haywagon a thunderhead above suddenly dumped a torrent of rain on us and our premium timothy and clover-dried hay. In a fit of anger, he stopped the horses, stood upright, all six feet two inches, stared at the sky, and shouted, "You dorry no good son-na-ma-betch!"

Years later while dying at the Mayo Clinic, his battered old gray Fedora hat deliberately covering the portrait of Jesus hanging on the hospital wall, he took my wife's trembling agnostic hands in his and with teary blue eyes asked her, "Ked-dee, you think maybe we see each other again sometime, someplace?" She sobbed, "Yes Mike, I just know we will."

In later years in a nursing home my mother lay dying. As I bent down to kiss her good-bye, I said, "Ma, I'm sure we'll see each other again somewhere, someplace." "Eddie," she whispered, "when you're dead you're dead, you rascal you!" which was a favorite expression she often used, from a popular song in the late nineteen twenties.

My wife's mother died when she was five. Left to grow up with five siblings and a hardworking, free-spirited blacksmith father, she began to question her church's teachings. By the time she finished college she considered herself a "fallen-away Catholic." We were married in an Episcopal chapel only because the minister, old "beady eyes," was her friend and we both thought city hall was a bit tacky—I think.

We have three sons, none of whom were baptized. We'd rather be wrong than hypocritical. Besides, we felt they should be able to make up their own minds when educated as to which faith, if any, they wished to join. We tried to make sure that wherever we lived they attended Sunday School. Katie and I did formally join the Unitarian church in part because they had such a great school for kids. They studied all the major religions of the world and preached that there was no one and only religion, just do good and be good.

All three sons are married to church-going German Catholic wives. The good Lord has a sense of humor!

As for me, my views are shaped by my education in physics, my lifelong work with engineers, and my trust in Ohm's Law. However, I believe I'll stick with my Guardian Angel, Chief Wildwind, who rides alongside of me always, and someday someplace someone will figure this all out for me.

Blue Eyes

He sat by the card table covered with homework and stared at me.
I pretended preoccupation with my book, but peripheral vision

locks on to his inquiring eyes. My head turns; I meet his gaze.
A shiver runs through me as I realize I am looking at the distinctive

blue eyes of my grandson, of my son, of my father, of myself. My

mother used to tell me my fathers' eyes were the color of the ageless
Adriatic sea near his birthplace. We have Adriatic blue eyes. The eye

genes must be dominantly strong, as all the progeny of Big Mike
have his eyes.

"What are you staring at, Nick?"

"Grampa, what did you write with when you were a little boy?"

"Number two pencils, mostly. No ballpoint pens then, just
regular pens with little ink pots sunk in our desktop."

"Grampa, how many words could you write before you had to
dip the pen in the ink pot?

"Nicky, I suppose thirty or forty."

"That's a lot of words, Grampa."

"Well, maybe it was fifteen or so."

"But, Grampa, why did you first say thirty or forty?"

"Nicky, sometimes your Grampa exaggerates or embellishes."

"Grampa, that's what my teacher says I do, too!"

The Fireplace

The burning logs capture my eyes;

I cannot look away.

I stare at the flames leaping amidst glowing coals,

They dance a yellow orange ballet

Behind the proscenium arch

Of Tennessee stones.

They speak to me in word pictures.

I wish to answer and cannot.

The soft hiss of the burning elm stokes my

Memory. A young boy is told by his mother

Why it's called a piss elm. A saint once peed

On burning elms and put the fires out. Since then

All elms sound like they are peeing when they burn.

Forgotten Feelings

Is there no one left who remembers the feeling of plowing a virgin meadow behind a team of straining draft horses? They pull in perfect unison, needing little guidance. The reins rest behind your head on your shoulders while each hand clutches an oak handle of a worn

and weathered single-bottom steel plow. It slices cleanly through the reluctant but yielding sod, which follows the curvature of the moving, shiny blade and turns, belly up, a furrow. I guide with my hands while my left foot walks on meadow and my right foot on the newly formed

ridge, tamping and tucking the earth into a red-brown symmetry. Red wing blackbirds follow us, feasting on earthworms whose whole world has suddenly changed. This sound of plowing is unlike any other sound. It is the mixture of horses' hooves straining and pulling,

with tails swishing away persistent flies; the sonance of earthen sod being cleanly sliced and turned. A not-so-occasional rock erupts from the plow's prow heralded by the grating screech of steel scraping stone. No airplanes roar overhead; gravel roads had not

been replaced by ear-deafening freeways. These solitary sounds are constant and unruffled. The rustle of poplar leaves joins the buzzing of pesky green flies to form muted background music. Pleasant memories; distillate left from the dregs of fatigue, boredom,

—and loneliness.

The Promise

The old woman's eyes asked my blessing. Too long
alone, too young to die, the promise of new life appeared

as wildflowers in barren soil. Prince Charming had arrived, her
salvation, her future. Everything her dead husband was not. A

nondrinker who talked and laughed with her, unlike father, quiet,
alone, lost in reading. She would have joy; he liked people,

traveling, visiting, not reading. He wished marriage, this retired
farmer. She could garden again, cook and keep house. Warm,

comfortable, compatible, companionship to journey's end. On
father's deathbed a promise was asked. Give care to her, watch over
her. I

did not. What appeared to be was not.

Matchless

The soft ocean breeze blows red hair
over queenly ears. Waves break over jet black

sand and bubbles disappear with water's sigh.
You stop for a shell with wonder, reluctant

to leave, taking it with you.
Both unique in Creation's spontaneity,

the shell and you, beauty and oneness.
The horizon leaves with darkness.

Stars appear, your celestial quilt. You walk
in sinking sand with your aloneness.

SES-TI-NA: Poem having six six-line stanzas and a three-line envoy: the end words of the first stanza are repeated with progressively changed order in the other five stanzas and are included finally in the envoy.

Grandpa

The early Autumn sun caresses the worn out barn.
Overhead geese fly crabwise to the wind,
their incessant cries lift eyes upward to the sky.
Green and gold semaphores twist softly in popple trees,
sending urgent messages, the voices of leaves
telling him what he already knows, telling Grandpa

the tarpaper roof leaks and it's getting late, Grandpa.
Nails have popped loose from the beatings of wind.
Pine boards, warped and curled, of once mighty trees
now thirst for red paint. Come fix up the barn
before winter blows in, before snow starts to fall, say the leaves.
Under the hayloft old cracks beckon, come see the sky,

come see the geese, come see the clouds in front of the sky.
The wood pile beckons alongside the trees;
dull, dry, and blanched from summer's wind,
ready to split with your double-bit axe, Grandpa,
ready to wheelbarrow away from the leaves
past summer's garden and next to the barn.

67

Tamarack and cedar stacked by the barn,
get ready for winter, cold days ahead, Grandpa.
Cowbells still sing among pastures and trees,
Guernseys and Holsteins with rears to the wind,
chewing their cuds beneath the cool sky,
soon to be grazing among fallen leaves.

What think, Grandpa, when will the leaves
fall, when will it freeze? When will the cows go into the barn,
away from the cold and the coming gray sky?
Can cows dream of spring and alfalfa, old Grandpa,
of cooling themselves in the creek by the trees
while letting their coarse hairs rise up in the wind?

Soon silent snowfalls will drift from the wind
to bring cover and stillness on blankets of leaves.
Stark, dark limbs of harried trees
will stand silhouetted against the cold sky.
Autumn's curtain drops quickly, Grandpa.
Stop dreaming of youth and fix that old barn.

It's getting close to milking time; the sky
is getting dark. The windblown leaves still whisper and cling
to the branches of the trees. Grandpa walks slowly to the barn.

Going to Town

Mother is left alone Saturday mornings with her chores and
her dreams. Pa shaves with the straight edge that cuts whiskers
and flesh, impatient for the journey to begin and to end.
He carefully dresses in suit and tie. The black patent-leather shoes
glisten. The gray hat covers his thinning hair, someone might

meet him who remembers. Soon sidelong glances into reflective
glass store windows will reward him with the image he once was.
He sings when driving, accompanied by the unrhythmic undulation
of our dark green Graham Paige automobile. A mechanic once told
him a steady engine is bad. We tell him car sickness isn't good, either.

We three sit in front with rear seats removed to make room for
gunny sacks of potatoes which he will exchange at Signe's store for
flour, canned goods, Bull Durham tobacco, and a Snicker bar we
divide. The once fancy, mottled, green-velvet upholstery, now worn
and dusty, smells of middlings, cow feed, and corn. Once a
powerful, eye-catching, high speed, touring car, now a truck.

The Stove

Naturally for the rest of my life I long
to see her. She leans over the dull black stove,

whose yearning for split birch never slackens, but settles
for inferior popple. First to rise in darkness and quiet,

to breathe new life into dying white coals; last to leave
in evening's black silence, firebox stuffed and damper closed.

Her face glows, she sings. Her head is covered with cloth,
nunlike in whiteness, lest a stray hair falls into her

mashed potatoes. Her strong, slender arm swirls the masher
around and around the large metal pot, in search of hidden lumps

hiding in foam feathery fare, injecting love and care,
unlike today's blender; lonely, sterile, automatic.

"Get some more wood, the wood box is empty. So is
the bucket, get some more water. The slop pail is full,

so empty the slop pail; the pigs are hungry, the calves
must be, too. So put your book down, get moving, I'm busy."

I wondered why the wood box was always empty
and the slop pail always full, why the rusty red pump

in the damp, rotted pump house squealed and squeaked,
protesting the loss of its cool, clear spring treasure.

Comfort fills the small kitchen, mixing with trust and love.
The burning firewood sings and crackles its approval.

Only This Hour

I. Aloneness satisfies until one becomes lonely.
We search for space as hunger cries for food,
only to rebuff it when gorged.
Want wets desires and wanes when satisfied as
waterfalls become placid pools. Time shrinks as
the journey races toward oblivion.
The sun is dying; we take no heed.
Friends depart faster than new ones appear.

II. New life enters amidst memories of those
no longer here. The Olympic torch is passed
in birthing, replete with genes and DNA,
assuring continuity to the mysterious ongoing
voyage. The aged grandfather reflects on the twin
infants in his arms; wide-eyed, wiggling, drooling,
a little boy, John, a red-haired girl, Katie.
How old will they be when he leaves?
What will become of them; what will become of him?

There truly is only this hour.

Poems About Age

On the Age Thing

In the March 21, 1994, issue of *The New Yorker* magazine a series of articles relating to Americans' love of movies includes a piece by Harold Brodkey which addresses the popularity of actors and actresses, and how this popularity wanes with the eventual and inevitable aging of the film stars despite the best efforts of the art of cosmetic enhancements. The actress you never liked dies, and in death evokes praise as though expiration sifts and strains dullness and mediocrity as one sheds layers of clothing when coming in from the cold. After a good deal of reflection and thought I have to agree with the general tenets of the author's conclusion; i.e., old age sucks!

I would add, however, that old age is a bummer not only for the rich and famous, but for all of us who, for better or for worse, depending on one's philosophical and/or religious outlook, have escaped near prime-of-life death and have entered the final phase, the autumnal segment, of the life span. I find it interesting that so many books, magazine articles, plays, and lectures are devoted to aging, and most have a common thread. The similar theme tells us not to fight aging, but to relax and enjoy it. Adapt to the changes that occur. One is as old as one feels, so feel young and good and you will be young and good. If one believes aging is undesirable, it certainly will be. Keep busy. Get involved with organized senior activities. Give back to society. Meet new people. Play bingo.

I suspect that the ones who tell others this are either slogging through the swamps of senility themselves or are lying through their dentures. Possibly they are in fear of projecting an image to their juniors of not being "good soldiers," and therefore, pitiable.

I have been young and I have been old. Young is better. It is far more preferable to worry about the results of a job application than to await the results of the latest PSA blood test—are the numbers stable, or are they rising? Are the bad cells sleeping, or are they awake and eating you? Car payment concerns disappear when compared with deterioration of eyes and ears. Thank God it's Friday beats the hell out of what should I do today. How one longs to hear the roar of the Mixmaster drowning out the sports scores you've been waiting to hear. There is nothing lonelier than an empty house full of memories and no calls waiting on the telephone.

When one is young a month is as a year. The retired wonder why the seasons are as shooting stars across the galaxy of time. They cannot comprehend that time has shrunk, as have they. If only one's life could be as a VCR, with replay, fast forward, and, most importantly—pause.

Not Whether

Not whether I will grow old,

I am old.

Not whether I'll get cancer,

I've had cancer.

Not whether I'll marry,

I've been married.

Not whether I'll be rich or poor,

I've been rich and poor.

Not whether I'll have Salvation,

Now that's a tough one.

Left to right: Dr. Joe Grayden, DDS; Ed Grayden Sr.;
Dr. Ed N. Grayden, MD; Dr. Tom Grayden, MD

Graduation Day

We sit in rows of foldup chairs atop the green lawn; graduates, with black gowns and caps, like crows and grackles in a harvested oat field, only quiet and attentive. Learned speakers are introduced to us; each speaks, then sits down as the scholastic ritual unfolds as it has every year for the last century. Why must my mind wander when profundity reigns?

I must be the oldest person on this campus. I should feel self-conscious, but I don't. With black masks we would all look the same. Under bed covers with lights out, none would be old, none would be ugly, and none would be lonely. The speaker has a scarlet hood.

The sky keeps getting blacker—when will the rain start? The forecast was sunny. A small aircraft overhead with sputtering engine searches for a runway. Poor bastard! Scan the instruments, switch fuel tanks, magnetos, start a glide, keep control. My sphincter starts to pucker and tighten in unconscious syncopation with the one 2,000 feet overhead. Relax, the engine comes to life; it's born again. Would I want to be born again?

The speakers are through; your classmates are inspired and ready to embark on yet another pathway. My new pathway seems strewn with the boulders of reality. Where are the dreams that used to be? Are they all used up or just rusted out from sitting around and waiting? I'll look harder; there's got to be some left up ahead. Maybe I'll find one that someone didn't want because they weren't smart enough to know what a good dream is.

Names are being called. Black figures rise, cross the stage, shake hands, get their Master's degree, return, and sit. We beat the rain.

The Last Lap

Mary Oliver closes her poem, "The Summer Day," with the questions, "Doesn't everything die at last, and too soon? Tell me, what is it you plan to do with your one wild and precious life?"

I wear these questions as I wear my clothes; each blood test, every x-ray, brings me a precious extension which must not be used as a Kleenex wet with tears. The sunrise of a new season brings experience with new friends amidst continuity and comfort of old ones.

I see shrieking, loving grandchildren at the airport run to me. I see their hair turning into golden red harmony, a legacy of their beautiful grandmother.

What new learning journeys await me? Who are they, new friends not yet met? How exciting, the new motorcycle with dreams of Sturgis next fall, alongside my son, Joe. Key West beckons in January, a seminar to attend on Elizabeth Bishop.

The old Gibson guitar has new strings; I sing with Willie. "Yesterday's dead and tomorrow is blind and I live one day at a time."

The rocking chair must bide its time; I always hated slippers.

Skiing on Aspen Mountain

Skiing on Aspen Mountain

Boughs sag steeply under heavy snow whose
whiteness narrows eyes from mountain sun.

I hear stillness broken by the humlike gurgle of the
steel cable moving through icy air. The chairlift

passing through tower pulleys elicits a rhythmic clacking sound
as if unseen sentinels were recording my skyward journey,

reporting me to Master Control. The computer knows my age, it
knows my odds. Today the lift ticket is half-price; tomorrow it's
free.

Could this be the last run of the day? Of the season? Of my life?
I think these thoughts calmly; my runs have gone well.

The muffled sound of a down-jacketed body slamming into
the packed powder snow raises my eyes uphill to

witness the released skis flying askew, while the skier rolls
"ass–over–teakettle" down the steep slope, finally resting

motionless and spread-eagled. A young skier runs
to him, bends over him. He hears his

father's cry from afar: "Wait for the ski patrol! Don't touch him! Americans sue everyone!"

I look downward and see distant peaks; how long have they been there? Where will they go?

Time stands still in the Rocky Mountains
where summits kiss the sun.

Status Report

The sun must set or the stars will cry. Days come and go, as do weeks, months, and years. There is no time out; adapt on the fly, death stops nothing except those that die. Seasons change, the old grow older. Friends say good-bye and families scatter. Junk mail still seeks her, junk mail and I. Chile's orphans and giant blue whales, abandoned forever, the pleas are not heard.

"How am I doing?" I'm asked all the time. "Just fine, hangin' in there, life must go on." Cruise ships and ski trips, movies and plays. Dinners and lunches crowd out the days. The facade grows thicker with the passing of time. It is fakement adorned with fun and laughter, keeping sadness shackled and hidden as spoiled wine in a cellar no one descends to.

As I lie alone in my bed, I remember the quote, "O sleep, that sometimes shuts out sorrow's eye, steal me awhile from mine own company."

Thanksgiving 1997

It is Thanksgiving Day in Aspen, Colorado, and once again the ski
season starts.
The cloudless sky allows the fiery brilliance of the mid-morning
sun to welcome
One and all to the glorious snow-blanketed mountain peaks whose
beauty defies
Description. The annual pilgrimage to Snow Mass Mountain has
begun with

Skiers of all ages milling about in colorful clothing, banging their
boots with
Poles, laughing, some with stocking hats and colored goggles, others
with dark
Sunglasses, all waiting impatiently. Celebrities mingle without both-
ersome fans.
Kevin Costner blows his nose and no one stops to stare. Robert
McNamara,

Bald, without glasses, without goggles, laughing heartily. Probably a
Mekong
Delta joke. Better that he wear a full-length ski mask and sackcloth
jeans.
The new quad lift starts to move upward and the line begins to
move. Ski
attendants examine each skier for proof they have paid, no longer
using sticky

Lift tickets; now they brandish a ray gun toward encoded pieces of
   plastic
Attached to ski jackets like clerks in a supermarket pricing your
   groceries.
A beep signifies you have paid and you shuffle ahead to the launch
   pad, poles in
One hand, eyes over shoulders, tense, awaiting the swiftly moving
   seat you will

Sit upon. No time to slip or ask questions. The reassuring feel of the
   seat and
Backrest tells you your voyage to the top has begun. Snow covered
   aspen and fir
Form guidelines on each side of the ascending chairlift as if they
   were guardian
Sentinels standing at attention as dignitaries ride through. Soon a
   majestic view

Thrills your senses and you can see a hundred miles in every direc-
   tion. One
Marvels at the montage of muted colors, shades of greens and
   browns entwined
With subdued pinks and grays, summits topped with whipped
   cream. Suddenly
You are a mile higher than when you started and thoughts turn to
   leaving this lift

While it moves. The sign at the start of this last segment told me
This High Alpine run is a double-black diamond, but groomed. A
   tiny shack

Looms ahead with signs warning you to tilt up your ski tips and
   prepare yourself.
I suddenly wonder why they let me ski free just because I'm old.
   What

Do their computers know that I don't? Poles at the ready, you shove
   yourself off
The chair and out of the way as your skis touch the snow-covered
   platform. You
Glide away from the lift and get ready for the challenge of skiing
   down the
Mountain. But first, a long drink of the views and maybe a sense of
   immortality.

Poems About Other Things

Cabin on Lake Sylvia

Cabin Opening

My cabin lies inert as though, from winter's slumber, Sleeping
    Beauty
awaits a wake-up kiss. It is the first spring visit to Lake Sylvia and the

annual ritual once again begins. What has happened here since last
    fall's
closing? It looks so abandoned and desolate. I hear voices asking
    where

have I been, and what have I done? I've been visiting grandchil-
    dren and
searching for sun. I've been skiing the snow slopes though too old to

ski. Cutting up firewood and watching it burn, drinking red wine
    while
recalling old memories. Observing how jokes and old stories give
    way to

talk of blood pressure, strokes, and prostate treatment. And count-
    ing the
days until Lake Sylvia awakens. A strong north wind gives birth to
    ice-water
waves tumbling and chasing each other to my cabin's bleak shore-
    line. No

one is here. Not even a robin or a chipmunk. Silence is total and
blankets

all. I am the first to return. The starkness of leafless trees contrasts
with
the dullness of winter-weathered pine and pale green cedar. Layers of

languid lackluster leaves, cold and sodden, await my rake. Plots of
rumpled
black dirt cry out for redemption by fertilizer, flower bulbs, and
the hoe.

Two weeks ago I flew low over the region's lakes to see if the ice
had left.
Minnetonka, Waconia, Buffalo, all were ice-free, but not Sylvia. It
was an

oasis of solid ice. Every year it's the the last lake to be free of winter's
freeze. I wonder why. Maybe the Ice God lives here and hates to
leave.

Each spring as I stand on this hill overlooking the cabin, the trees,
and the
lake. The scene is the same. And if some year I do not return, there
will be

yet another to stand and stare, to wonder.

The Apple Tree

There is an apple tree in my backyard which I hardly ever noticed. It was hard to see from my window; it was surrounded and hidden by tall, majestic elms, oaks, and maples. I wonder why Katie planted it there those many years ago. When I mowed around it I wished it would die; it was in my way and looked so scrawny, sickly, and stunted. Small wonder, with a thick forest hogging all the sunlight, water, and love. I never asked her why.

Plants, trees, flowers, color schemes, all were in her domain and never challenged. Last year I had a tree man come out and remove dead trees and limbs, to prune and to trim. Today I noticed the apple tree is clearly visible. It has grown tall and is flowering with a thick, glorious gown of pale pink petals. It has appeared front and center in nature's theater in the woods, a new prima ballerina.

It is saying, "You've missed me all these years. I've waited for you to see."

The Lake Place

It is noon; the wail of a loon intrudes on leaves jostling in concert with blue gray-waves trying to whitecap, not quite making it. The moody backside of the passing weather front shifted the winds to come from the northwest while pushing the low cumulus clouds and intermittent rain showers slowly and reluctantly out of the area. The loons and the leaves have returned from winter's exile as they do every year. This constancy amidst aging and change reassures and calms; a tow rope to long past memories and events, to nostalgia.

Tomorrow's Friday will be nice, greeting the start of a beautiful summer weekend at Lake Sylvia. The roar of motorboats will intertwine with the joyful shrieks of children who water ski and dive from floating platforms and docks into the clear cool water.

The sights and sounds are as a digital disc player programmed to repeat after the last selection, with no sign of age or usage to mar one's ingrained memories. Nor does it matter that the audience changes with the passing of decades. It remains a transitory observer.

Someone today is weeding their flower garden, or adding on a deck, or admonishing a dog. Only the names change. Ownership remains an illusion.

A Plane Wreck

I saw a plane wreck in the news today, metal bowels strewn
between virgin popple scarring a snow-white hill of spent taconite.

The silence of twenty passengers and crew joins the quiet of the
    forest,
and throughout the land there is sadness and wonderment.

Why these people, one asks? They had lives to live, loved ones to be
with, plans to complete, a journey to end. Gleaming metal shines in

the dawn's dim light, crippled, torn, and spent, returning to the womb
of earth from which it came. Once proudly soaring over clouds and

mountains, now resting silently, a broken coach of death. It matters
not what plans were made by these unfortunate souls. It matters only

to those alive who ponder and ask why, then realize our stay is brief;
how close we are to die.

Lake Sylvia Storm

It's a funny feeling to be alone at a lake during a storm. I am uneasy
and worry how long it will last; what damage will occur.

A June tornado made some calls last night, here and there,
hop-scotching across lakes and farms and little towns,

not pausing to visit me; perhaps next time. The whitecaps have
left and the lake water remains as an unironed shirt quick dried

with high heat. Low cirrus clouds, rear-guard action for
pissed-off retreating cumulus, slink toward the horizon

leaving a troubled and hazy sky, unsure of itself. Leaves
on branches, survivors of blitzkrieg winds, become quiescent;

they take count of their casualties. It was the longest
day of the year, and it hardly stayed at all. The thunder-soaked

wind is no longer heard; sunset begins its glorious ritual, where
heart and mind blend into one question mark: Where is she?

She was here with me two summers ago clapping her
hands as the sun descended behind the proscenium

arch of the lush green horizon, remembering Key West
docks and youthful sun worshippers. Does she still see

sunsets, whitecaps, and wind-blown tree limbs? Or is she air,
seeing nothing; feeling all?

Spring Break

It's spring break at Fort Myers Beach in 1992.
Pelicans pitch and yaw as they waddle on concrete

casements, calm but intense, waiting
for nearby fishermen to catch fish or lose bait.

Fat tourists on anchored cruise ships tan beneath
large hats while lying on beach cots. They sip

cool drinks brought by thin third-world waiters. A large
hoist and derrick stands tall on the sand beach, imperious,

ready to launch a bronzed scholar earthward to
kiss death's cheek gently and return skyward by

the bungee umbilical cord tied to his heels. Gold-toned
women walk gingerly over hot sand with stamp sized

swimsuits whose thongs disappear deep between rounded
buttocks. The single solitary road parallels the beach and

serves as pathway to endless traffic undulating in a stop-
and-go pattern like some unending multicolored caterpillar.

Condominiums rise tall to split Gulf winds while cave dwellers
sit high on patios and dream of youth in snow without sickness.

Night's darkness brings silent bars and dance floors to life.
Ear-deafening music blocks reality and pain. Bodies gyrate,

pass, and touch while bottles and glasses tinkle and clink.
The world is now; life passes never to return.

Leaving Loons

It is late September and autumn leaves form a border color mon-
tage around
limpid Lake Sylvia. Two loons singing loony tunes, wings flailing, feet

scrambling, running on water, unable to fly, not unlike an overweight
seaplane trying to break water's sucking grip, practicing for the real
thing

soon to come, practicing to break Lake Sylvia's bond. It will happen
as sure
as Lindbergh's fragile, staggering takeoff led him to cross the Atlantic,
so too

will the loons somehow rise awkwardly above these resplendently
beautiful
treetops, Nature's silent poetry, and head south. Winter's haven is a

beacon where water never hardens and fish-filled bays have the
welcome
mat out. Here they will wait for spring's green light and without
sextant,

compass, or satellite positioning, return to their birthplace, return to
Lake
Sylvia, home of the loon.

Vine Hill Leaves

Resplendent beaches in Hawaii bathe in sunlight and moonbeams,
Pacific sunsets give way to Southern Cross star-kissed skies.

Snowcapped Rockies, remote and unreal, remain imperious and
    majestic.
The Monterey coast boasts whitewater waves assaulting mammoth
    cliffs

And pock-marked rocks. Nature's beauty is throughout the world. Yet
Here alongside my home the annual autumn wonder starts at
    Highway

Seven and fills the three-mile stretch of winding, undulating blacktop
Called Vine Hill Road. Each October ushers in a pageant of beauty
    that

Rivals all anywhere. The leaves are changing their colors! Each day I
Watch this breathtaking transition take place with so many subtle

Expressions that art museums would die for. Maples, oaks, bass-
    wood, and
Elm crowd and encroach the meandering road; all have their own
    special

Leaf, each has its shade of golds and yellows, of reds and orange.
    Scarlet
Sumac vies for attention and fails. Each new day brings tiny shifting
    in the

Gaiety of the kaleidoscope. For forty years I have observed and
    absorbed
this beauty and given thanks to have shared all this with loved
    ones, and

To know that every year the eternal leaves return.

Winter

The story of winter is always somehow the story of snow.
Northland transformation; white covers all. Distant sounds

clarified as nature's boom box magnifies train-travel din
with woodpeckers' staccato. Metamorphis is simultaneous

with first snowfall. Are they plowing and sanding yet, we ask. Be
careful, the light flakes join together and become heavy blankets

or shrouds for the overzealous shoveler with cardiac overtones. The
aged residue of fall is erased as chalk from a blackboard. Sunlight's

brightness, enhanced and intensified by snow-crystal mirrors, is a
giant
stagelight to the proscenium arch of a newborn world. We recall the

Armistice Day blizzard with abandoned cars and stranded travelers.
With each passing year those snowdrifts grow, soon to tower over

telephone poles; one huge Minnesota avalanche. Precious snow
scenes burn permanent molds in memories for future casting of

remembered moments. A three-year-old rolling and stomping
in satiny snow, arms flailing, falling and rising, screaming and

laughing, red cheeked with runny nose. So brief the magic; so fragile the moment.

Beauty

Three score years ago he labored in the small Midwestern town, far from his family, apart from his paintings; an uncommon common laborer, grateful for his daily pay. His task was to wrap and insulate the large steampipes with asbestos wrap, unknown killer then, asbestos rolls shipped on large wooden spools, strong heavy spools, whose core was a rough block of solid birch stronger than iron. He was skilled in watercolors and oils, but they were far away. The birch block was there. He had his sharp knife, he would carve.

The two-foot sculpture rests on a marble table in our home. It was a present from Elof Wedin, the immigrant Minnesota artist, now long dead, to my wife, his former student. It was his only sculpture. This piece of birch has watched me for over twenty years as I pass it by daily. Occasionally I stop and stare in wonder. I feel its presence; the feeling of never being alone in the room.

Such sadness and magnificence radiate from this face. Deep lines cut unevenly through the tight natural grain unblemished by stain or knot, projecting weariness and resignation. The simplicity of the few strokes which bring forth mouth and beard is at variance with the complexity of expression. The long, curved aquiline nose, start-ing from hewn eyebrows, droops down between closed eyes that cry. Atop the head rests the crown of thorns.

The Pileated Woodpecker Is Back

The powerful two-inch beak hammers at the frozen suet on the bird feeder. Beyond stand winter's leafless trees; tall oaks, maples, elms, and basswood whose snowy limbs and tangled branches form a confused montage of wood and clouded sky. Its blows trumpet echoes throughout house and woods, announcements of life amidst stillness.

Nature's leaden backdrop contrasts sharply with this most beautiful bird in these woods; the rarest, largest, and most wary. The crescent cap atop head so red is its magnificent banner. It scans sectors of the sky between bites. It is watchful and nervous, as if at any moment something will swoop down from above and hurt it.

For years Katie and I watched in quiet wonder, this pageant played by our shy and welcome visitor. This is the first day I have seen this magnificent bird in almost three years. It disappeared when Katie died. I thought it might have died also. Maybe it did, and is now back eating suet again, telling me to get on with life, but to also scan the sky.

Two Hearts

Did you know there are really two hearts, not one? The left heart
    and the
right heart. Maybe a new name, then, is better. Like "heart assem-
    bly" or

"heart complex." The right heart takes old, tired, worn-out blood
    and
pumps it to the lungs where it is cleansed and rejuvenated with
    oxygen from

our breathing. The left heart takes this born-again blood and
    pumps it
throughout the body to nurture, succor, and sustain the system that
    enables

life to exist. One hundred thousand beats per day pumps 1,800 gal-
    lons of
blood. A person of eighty years has over 52 million gallons of blood
    course

their veins. The heart should not be a symbol of love but rather a
masterpiece of nature. When bypassed with a mechanical pump,
    emotions

and feelings still remain. Love and pragmatism are governed by two
little
spirits that frolic throughout our bodies, Hans and Heidi. Heidi
tells my

body to go for it, take your best shot, the world is for the taking.
Hans
says you've worked hard enough, play it safe, coast and enjoy. Hans is

always right; Heidi is more fun.

Why?

Why does that loon find our bay from a thousand miles away?
But it does.

Why can't water tilt?
Jello does.

Why don't airplanes drop to earth?
Rain does. A rock would.

Why is a banana yellow and curved? Why not straight and red?
A pepper is.

Why do cancer cells multiply and eat you up?
They sometimes do. Why sometimes?

Why do loved ones die while you live?
Why does God call if God called?

Why can't I understand God and Jesus and all that stuff?
Others do.

October

October in Minnesota is a nervous, jumpy month; apprehension and
foreboding greet each new day. Weather reports and El Niño alarm
    me,

Winter is skulking and lurking nearby; a new snow shower yester-
    day
confirms. Transition has started. I view with sadness the beauty of
    my tall

red Salvias, survivors of summer's rabbits and hungry deer, now
    awaiting
the inevitable killing frost. Hopefully it will be a sudden macho
    frost. If it's

just a mild, wimpy one, I promised myself not to scurry around
    searching for
blankets to prolong life as these crimson beauties agreed to living-
    will

guidelines when planted; all have lived the good life giving me
    much
pleasure so I must let go; the death of these beautiful friends is
    imminent.

October's glorious leaves now fall to the ground leaving ghostly
   barren
branches looking down on yellow and gold earth blankets. These
   naked

limbs are as silent sentinels set against the inevitable Arctic siege
   soon to
begin, not soon to end.

Have water lines been drained?

Is the car winterized?

Will the snowblower work?

I can't find my long underwear anywhere.

Note in My Mail Box

I saw a notice to advance my clocks an hour;
Daylight savings is here again.

I saw brown stains from ice-jammed roof water,
Leaking through corners of my white kitchen
Ceiling. Another challenge lies ahead.

I saw a small, scrawny evergreen blowing in
The spring wind, shed of winter's ice and snow,
With thin, sickly boughs struggling for life,
Hoping the hungry deer have not grown taller.

I saw a stiff dried mouse under the basement
Laundry tub and felt death's closeness.

I saw a fast charging Jeep in my
Rearview mirror, swaying from side to side,
Trying to pass in a no-pass zone, cell phone
In ear. I felt the panic of a June bug in front of a chicken.

I saw the pileated woodpecker's red-headed
Beak beat its jackhammer staccato into
The aged oak. The bird, the tree, and I
Face another season.

Valentine

Valentine's Day sprouts heartfelt tributes like hordes of locusts in a summer field of purple clover. Restaurants

and drugstores, meat markets and gas stations all cry out to remember her this special day. A card or a box of

candy is fulfillment, a soothing balm to placate a gnawing need, a void deepened each day of the year

to be erased by the annual Hallmark incantations. Birthdays, deaths, battles, events of note, all deserve

their one day of commemoration. One's love of another deserves better. Love is the air we breathe, the sights

we see, the sounds we hear. Love rests in us when we sleep and greets us when we awake. Love needs no

wake-up call. It is the woven fabric of caring and concern that binds one to another forever.

The Evergreen

The dense green thicket blocks eye and hand, wind and rain.
Sheltered haven to the glorious cardinal, playground of mice

and chipmunks. Yesteryear's planting was a tiny shrub; now,
a majestic cone. The contractor said it must go, quick grist

for his hungry chainsaw. And yet I rush to save from oblivion
this fruit of Creation, too soon for landfills' lonely grave.

It now rests at the edge of our woodlot; scrawny, scraggly,
sickly, and alone, like a transplanted immigrant. Deer

have feasted on its limbs leaving a bare skeleton, shorn
of verdant needles. Stray dogs complete its ignominy.

Still Life

The Monet print turned his brain into mindful images of her.

She had been an accomplished artist and

Her still life paintings give life to the lonely

Walls of his silent home.

They greet him every morning

And say goodnight as he crawls into bed.

He wonders if she still paints;

Does she use watercolors, or oils,

Or wisps of clouds colored by a rainbow?

Onward Downward

I have lived my life in the greatest of times;
No wonder I wish not to leave.
The trip's been superb
and I'd like to stay on.
Is our planet better or worse?

The Buck Rogers backpack still isn't here
And the freeways really need help.
Cold fusion power is still down the road
Oh my, what a road it will be.

I wonder why sickness and hunger remain,
With all of these wonders of time.
With most of us still are hate, fear, and greed,
Inherited traits they must be.
They were here as a child;
They'll be here when I'm gone.
So what does this tell me today?

There were Hitler and Stalin and FDR,
Each saying that his was the way.
Millions agreed and millions died
And we still have hate, greed, and fear.

Governance has shown it's a questionable
God that one must continually doubt.
Religions abound with promises, promises.
Status quo now, Nirvana in the hereafter.
Where are the watersheds in music, art, and writing?
I don't recall a new Beethoven or Shakespeare.

Another lifetime would be another lifetime.

Starlight

I was told that the star I see is not there.

I am just looking at the light it discharged before it disappeared.

But where could the star have gone?

Next someone will tell me that my guardian angel, Chief Wildwind,

is not guarding me anymore, that he left with the star.

To order additional copies of this book,
please send full amount plus $4.00 for
postage and handling for the first book and
50¢ for each additional book.

Send orders to:

Galde Press, Inc.

PO Box 460
Lakeville, Minnesota 55044-0460

Credit card orders call 1–800–777–3454
Phone (612) 891–5991 • Fax (612) 891–6091
Visit our website at http://www.galdepress.com

Write for our free catalog.